A Little Story About How To Get **BI**

Always Be Looking For STARS

HOW LEADERS CAN HIRE THE RIGHT PEOPLE WITH THE RIGHT PROCESS

JERRY PHILLIPS

INDIE BOOKS INTERNATIONAL

ISBN-13: 978-1-947480-95-7
Library of Congress Control Number: 2020900166

Designed by Joni McPherson, mcphersongraphics.com

INDIE BOOKS INTERNATIONAL, INC.
2424 VISTA WAY, SUITE 316
OCEANSIDE, CA 92054
www.indiebooksintl.com

CONTENTS

PREFACE

This book is a fable to illustrate the need to always be looking for rock stars and have a process to attract and hire the right people for the role.

A little history for context: When I helped launch the DeWalt brand of power tools at Black and Decker, our fear wasn't whether we would grow the business. The fear was could we maximize the growth. Our challenge was not just taking share in the market we targeted, but having enough quality people to support the growth. We developed a recruiting process that produced a stellar team of sellers and marketers. Our growth was legendary.

As I worked with other companies, I found the process for finding talent to be hit or miss. The process was random, based on who was doing the hiring. Interviewing was haphazard as well. When I started working with clients on the development of their sales and marketing teams, I found the same challenges.

People are the lifeblood of a company. Without a clear process for recruiting, interviewing, hiring, and development of the team, finding the right talent is difficult and limiting your growth potential. We have worked with clients to develop a rigorous, disciplined process to hire and develop the needed rock star talent. My hope is this fable will help you find your rock stars.

Jerry Phillips
September 2019
Austin, Texas

1 ★★★★★

NINETY DAYS, OR ELSE

I'm so disappointed in you, Vincent. When I put you in charge as the CEO, I expected better of you."

Nobody wants to hear that type of criticism. Especially coming from Donna, the chairman of the board.

Vincent was no exception. He was widely recognized in the industry as a terrific strategist who was outstanding at execution. His secret was the development of his people.

But Donna was criticizing him for an undeserved misfortune. Over the past sixty days other companies had swooped in and taken the top three leaders from his team. All three had taken CEO roles, as a testament to Vincent's ability to develop his team.

However, Donna, the chairman of the board, saw it differently. She saw it as a threat to her personally, and to the income she was drawing off the company her father had founded. She saw Vincent as a threat, and also saw an opportunity.

The Power Play

Smyth Tools was an old-line manufacturing company that built parts for some of the biggest names in construction equipment. Donna's father, David, founded the company in the late 1960s and grew it from a small machine shop into a modern, automated facility that produced parts that were used on every major construction project in the world.

After fifty years of heading the company, David chose his oldest daughter to become the chairman.

Donna had little to do with the business, other than attending board meetings, but she was tough, and her father thought that was what the business needed now that he was stepping down. Donna saw it as a mandate. She was, by nature, a skeptic and acted in a narcissistic way. She trusted few people, and heartily enjoyed holding Vincent's "feet to the fire" on a multitude of things she saw as issues. If he was uncomfortable, she felt he would be more engaged in making money for the company. Making money for the company really meant making money for her. Donna had a very lavish lifestyle, and any threat to the income stream was a personal attack on her and her need for control.

Humble Roots

Vincent knew this when he agreed to take the CEO role, but he was an optimist by nature. He was certain he could lead the company and shield it from Donna's lack of leadership skills. He grew up "blue collar" in a large Italian family in a diverse working-class neighborhood in South Chicago. His father worked two jobs so his mother could stay home and raise the kids. Vincent knew the value of working hard and working smart. He was an above-average student in high school, and an outstanding wrestler that earned a scholarship to attend the University of Illinois where he majored in Industrial Engineering. In college he excelled both academically and as an athlete, earning dean's list recognition each semester, and earning all Big 10 honors after a dominating four years of wrestling. The only thing that kept him from becoming an Olympic wrestler was a shoulder injury suffered in a scuffle at a bar, during a team celebration after winning the Big 10 title. While he was initially devastated by the injury and his lack of judgment, he learned from the experience and moved on.

After graduation, Vincent began his career, working in a management training program for a large manufacturing company that ironically, is now a customer of Smyth Tools. He learned a great deal in the program. He learned all phases of manufacturing, but also was exposed to finance, sales, marketing, and operations beyond the manufacturing floor. He had an aptitude for leadership that saw him rise quickly through the program, and the company recognized it. They offered to pay for his MBA if he would make a three-year commitment to the company after he finished. He quickly agreed and entered the Kellogg MBA program at Northwestern University. Once he finished the program, he was armed with even more drive and ambition.

Vincent peaked in his role at the equipment manufacturer in another seven years, as a plant manager. The funnel narrowed as he grew into larger leadership roles and he was receiving weekly inquiries about his availability from multiple recruiters. He really wanted to continue to grow with the company and he was confident he could make a positive impact for more than the plant he was leading. He expressed his desire to become an operations leader across multiple facilities but was shut down by the VP of Operations. He was told he was too young and there were others with more seniority that would be ahead of him on the list. That day he took a call with the recruiter that was supporting a search for a VP of Operations at Smyth Tools.

After speaking with the recruiter, Vincent was whisked off to Houston to meet with the owner of Smyth Tools. While the interview was very different from those he had experienced in the past, he enjoyed talking with the founder of the company and decided he would make the move. In the next six months, Vincent and his wife, Maria, and their first son moved to Houston and he began his path to the CEO role at Smyth Tools.

Making Work And Life Adjustments

There were adjustments to make in both his business life and his personal life. Vincent had moved from a large corporate environment to a smaller, family run company. He had to adjust from the politics of a larger company to the politics of a family. He had to adjust to the new role, having responsibility for several plants in different locations, including one in Mexico. But the most difficult adjustment was personal. He now lived a great distance from where he and his wife had lived most of their lives. They had moved several times with the previous company, but it was just the two of them then. When they started their family, they were near both of their families and the support that goes with it. They now were on their own in a new city, and Vincent was traveling and buried in learning the culture and systems of Smyth Tools.

Though it was a stressful situation for both of them, it only made him better. Vincent thrived under pressure. Armed with the leadership training he had received from his past company, the knowledge he had gained from his MBA, and the experiences he had in all phases of the business, Vincent worked across all functions of the business to build a network of support that allowed him to increase productivity and align output with sales. The metrics he was goaled with were challenging, but he and his team were able to meet them.

His marriage grew even stronger as he leaned on his wife for her thoughts on business decisions and life decisions. He respected her ability to adapt to living in Houston and taking on the family leadership role as he took on the business leadership role. He realized he had some blind spots in his leadership skills, but she could see them when he could not. They were a strong team.

After four straight years of increasing productivity in operations, it was decided to elevate Vincent to the COO role. He had proven he could work across all functions and he was well respected.

The move was celebrated by the entire company. He was a powerful force, not only in the company, but in the entire industry. He was regularly quoted in trade magazines as an expert in building strong teams. He was outstanding at delegating assignments that helped his team members grow individually. He had been able to develop his team members and promote them to new roles.

Recruiters recognized this and his direct reports were constantly being recruited by other companies. With his guidance, some accepted new roles outside of Smyth Tools, but most stayed. They enjoyed working with Vincent and saw a great opportunity to continue to learn.

As his career grew, so did his family. He now had two sons and his wife was expecting their third child. They had put down strong roots in the community. Vincent had recruiters calling on a regular basis to inquire about his availability to join other companies. Some were interesting roles, others not as interesting, but he was always polite and open with the recruiters. He was on a path to be the CEO of Smyth Tools and he and his wife were in Houston to stay.

Two years after accepting the role as COO, David, the founder, came to Vincent with an offer. He was stepping down from running the business daily, and he wanted Vincent to take over as CEO. He was also stepping down as the chairman of the board. He was elevating Donna to the chairman role. He wanted to separate the roles, as this was the first time they had ever gone outside the family for a leader at this high level. While Vincent knew Donna was inexperienced and she had challenges in leadership, he was certain he could insulate the company from her musings, and he would have the role he had been preparing for his entire career. He accepted the offer immediately.

Growing Into The Role

Vincent's first few months as CEO were once again a flurry of activity, as expected. He was learning on the job. He was fine-tuning his ability to work with the board. He was getting through the challenges of working with Donna specifically. He had been able to promote from within the company to fill three key roles of leadership in sales, operations, and finance. His staff was strong, and the business continued to grow under his leadership. Even with a downturn in the economy, they were able to anticipate the effects and meet their goals. He identified initiatives to improve their mix of products, improve their mix of customers, and increase profitability.

He continued to be sought after as an industry expert, he participated in panel discussions and he was quoted in trade magazines. Late this last year, he had been interviewed by a reporter that wrote for *The Wall Street Journal* and there was a very complimentary article written about Smyth Tools and his leadership. That is when the real trouble started with Donna.

While the company was thriving and it was spinning off cash for the family, Donna wanted more. She had become very jealous of the publicity that Vincent was receiving. She wanted to be recognized as the person driving the company, not Vincent. While they had a workable relationship before the article, she now felt Vincent was a threat to her as chairman. She knew her father was very fond of Vincent and the work he was doing. She also knew, even though he was retired, her father still was the power in the boardroom. With the three key leaders being recruited away from Smyth, she saw this as her opportunity to bring Vincent in check and show him who really was in charge. So, she called him in to this meeting to set the rules, as she saw them, and to put herself in the spotlight.

"I'm so disappointed in you Vincent. When I put you in as the CEO, I expected better of you." Those words stung him. How did he get to this place? He had worked hard, and he had made moves that had made it a better company. He had a great staff that was so talented that they were recruited for CEO roles at other companies. That was as big a compliment as anyone can receive. He knew Donna was upset by the *Journal* article, but this, he didn't see coming.

He knew he had a talented staff and he was happy to support them in finding opportunities for them to run other companies. They had peaked in their ability to grow with Smyth Tools. He had taken great satisfaction in helping them develop their skills and the roles they took were well deserved. Yet now he was sensing that this was going to be an unpleasant conversation with Donna.

"What are you doing to replace your three key roles?" asked Donna. "I can't believe you let them leave. I'm told you even supported them leaving. Is that true?"

Donna was raising her voice and sounding more incredulous as she went through her prepared speech. She never waited for an answer to her question.

"You have ninety days to replace all three roles, or I will replace you."

SEARCHING FOR STARS

▶ **Losing your star team members is disruptive and expensive.**

▶ **Investing in their development allows you to retain your stars for a longer period of time.**

▶ **If you don't challenge your stars, they will find challenges elsewhere.**

2 ★★★★ ★

FREEZE, FLIGHT, OR FIGHT

Her words were still ringing in his ears. "Ninety days to replace all three roles, or I will replace you."

"She can't be serious, can she?" Vincent said to himself. "We have still performed with the internal team working as a bridge until we find the replacements for these key people. None of the internal team members are ready for the larger roles, and while it sent shock waves through the organization to lose such strong performers, the fact that they accepted roles as CEOs gave the organization a sense of pride, as well. These are top performers with great opportunities."

Vincent had worked to backfill the roles through a few different avenues but had yet to be successful. He had reached out to his personal and business network to find candidates, but had come up dry. These were big roles and needed strong candidates. He had used, through his human resources leader, some traditional job boards with little success. His internal candidates were too junior for backfilling the roles. They had potential, but they were not ready yet. What now?

Through the years, Vincent had relied on his wife Maria to help him with his major decisions. She was the yin to his yang, and she had an amazing ability to see through some of the obstacles that blocked his vision. They had always been a good team. Now he needed her more than ever. With that thought he set up dinner reservations at Carson's.

Carson's was an old school, five-star restaurant that they went to for celebrations of big events. The maître d' wore a tuxedo and the waiters were serious about the experience they helped provide. It was the perfect place to hold confidential conversations over great food and wine. When Vincent invited Maria to dinner, she knew that there was something big happening and she was excited to find out what they were celebrating. She made the call to her go-to sitter to watch the kids, even though at this point, the oldest felt he was too old for a babysitter.

As Strong As Your Support

Maria came from a large Italian family that lived close to Vincent's family. They had grown up together, although they didn't date until her sophomore year in college. They were friends first. She had always had a special place in her heart for Vincent and she saw the intensity and drive that he had from an early age. She was there for his high points in life, and she was there for the low points. After some long talks, she was the one who suggested he focus on business after his shoulder injury. He then poured his passion for competition into his career. She would support his career and put her career on hold over the next several years, but now she was settling in. She had put down roots in Houston and she had a community to support the family. She had earned her teaching certificate and was happily teaching first grade at the public school less than two blocks from their home. Whatever they were celebrating tonight at Carson's, she was hopeful it would not lead to a move to another city.

As they sat down to dinner, Vincent was nervous. Maria had always been supportive, but this was different. This was a crisis. This could disrupt their lives in a way neither had experienced before. He waited until the wine was poured before he started the deeper conversation. After a couple of sips of wine, he shared the news. Donna had given him an ultimatum: fill the roles in ninety days, or he was out. "How am I going to do this in ninety days?"

Maria was expecting a celebratory dinner, not this news. She was taken aback but remained calm. Vincent took her through the conversation with Donna in detail. He shared the process he had undertaken to fill the three key roles, with little or no success. Maria listened intently and took it all in—the stress her husband and partner in life was feeling, the slight sound of desperation in his voice, and the helplessness of being put in what he viewed as an impossible situation.

Once Vincent had finished his story, she took a sip from her wine, and she started to work. "Why do you think Donna is taking this hard stance now? The company is still performing beyond the goals that were set." Vincent had not thought about that. He was preoccupied with the threat to himself and the company.

As he processed her question, and Donna's motivation, he felt he had the answer. "She has picked another pony! She has always been power hungry and felt she was in her father's shadow. Now she sees an opportunity to replace her father's hand-picked successor and put her person in the CEO role. I'm certain she is looking for someone who won't challenge her ideas." This revelation put the conversation in a completely new light. This wasn't about performance; this was about power and politics.

It was obvious that Donna had been looking for something to act on for some time. Her father had chosen Vincent to become CEO without her input. He had made her chairman of the board, but she felt it was a toothless position, because her father still had the power of his presence. Now that her father was aging and less involved in the business, she could act and show Vincent and the world that this was her company.

The Challenge

Maria gathered her thoughts and decided it was time to challenge Vincent. He thrived on challenges, and his drive was triggered by them. While he needed time to process this, she knew he didn't have time. Ninety days was a short window to find the next great staff, and she needed to push him to act quickly. "Here's how I see this: you have three choices—freeze, flight, or fight. You can continue as you are and keep your search going as it is and see if Donna follows through on her threat. You get calls every week from recruiters, so you could entertain one of the offers that come from that. Or you can fight this and find the people you are looking for in the next ninety days. What do you want to do, Vincent?"

Freeze, flight or fight. It was certainly not Vincent's nature to freeze. He was action oriented from the time he was a young boy. That option was not appealing. He didn't want to let Donna decide his career. He wasn't one to run away from a challenge. While there were other CEO roles available to him, with some that would carry a lot more prestige, that wasn't what he was looking for, either. He loved the people, the product and the reputation of Smyth Tools. That left one thing: fight. But he wasn't certain how best to fight. He had exhausted all his traditional resources to find talent.

As he shared his thoughts with Maria, she offered her insight. "You have been receiving calls from recruiters for some time now. Have you thought of using one or all of them?"

Vincent had toyed with the idea of using a recruiter on his drive from Donna's office back to his, but he really didn't know the recruiters well, and he didn't really trust them. How could they find three top-caliber people, willing to move to his company in that short window of time? He put the idea of using a recruiter on the shelf for now. Was there someone he could find that he trusted to help him?

The Help

Vincent had sat on several industry panels on developing the right team and Maria remembered a specific panel that had Vincent still buzzing with excitement when he returned home. "Do you remember the panel you sat on for the Industrial Tooling Association back in August of last year? It was in Chicago at McCormick Place. You came home excited about the possibilities that the panel had shared."

Vincent thought for a moment and nodded his head yes. He remembered the panel and he remembered why he was excited. It wasn't the entire panel or even the subject that raised his interest. It was a fellow panel member, Carl.

Carl was an experienced consultant who had worked in the industry prior to opening his practice. He had opened his practice several years earlier after moving to a city he didn't want to leave. He thought it was Kansas City or Nashville—he couldn't remember specifics. He just knew that Carl had made an impression on him. He was strategic but was able to share execution plans as well. He talked about people being the lifeblood of a company and that their development was an absolutely critical part of a successful business.

Without strong people, a business was doomed to fail. The quote that had stuck with Vincent was "A players hire additional A players. B players never hire A players. They hire lesser talent so they don't feel threatened. If you have a B player in a lead role, you are setting your company up to fail." Vincent had thought about that quote and had used it to create a succession-planning process to determine where he had A players and B, or worse, players. He had started a development program for his top talent and a program to move his B players into more fitting roles or move them out of the company.

It had proven to be successful—so successful that his top leaders adopted the program he had developed, and now they were leading other companies. The only issue was he didn't yet have talent developed to the point that they could be replaced internally. Again, the pressure was on to fill the roles, and in a very short window.

As their entrées were served to them, Vincent and Maria took a few minutes to savor the aesthetics of the meal, as well as the wonderful aroma of the piping hot food. They took time to enjoy the moment. After a few bites of their food, they returned to the conversation.

He answered the question she had asked earlier about the panel he sat on in Chicago. Yes, he remembered the panel and no, it was not the event, it was Carl who energized him.

Maria was to the point, "Why don't you reach out to him and ask him for his insights?" It was a logical suggestion.

Adjusting His Thinking

Vincent was not the type of person who asked for help often and his mentors, while greatly appreciated, were few. He needed to adjust his thinking to look for help. He was a CEO, but it didn't mean he had to have all the answers, and it didn't mean he had to do everything on his own. David, the founder of Smyth Tools had been a mentor to him and had made a practice of reaching out to Vincent on a regular basis, but those conversations had slowed recently. It made him wonder if David was supporting Donna's bid to bring in a new CEO. He had his doubts. He felt the conversations had slowed because David was stepping away from the business and he was confident in Vincent's ability, not that he was ready to move him out. But, because Donna was David's daughter, Vincent didn't want to reach out to David and pull him into the "fight."

"I really don't know how to reach Carl. I spoke to him at the conference but didn't connect with him on LinkedIn or get his contact information. I can search for him on LinkedIn, I suppose. I'm hopeful he will remember me, and he will be available to help."

The next morning Vincent did find Carl's information through his LinkedIn search. He then sent a message to Carl, asking for a short telephone conversation to see if he had interest in helping him. The telephone call came in thirty minutes later. Carl had received the message and proactively called Vincent to follow up.

"Of course, I remember you, Vincent! You're the young superstar getting all the accolades for developing your staff and your company at the Industrial Tooling Association Conference. I really enjoyed your contributions to the panel discussion." Carl put Vincent at ease from the beginning of the conversation. It allowed him to speak freely, describing the situation at Smyth Tools and the pressure he was under to fill the three roles, now in eighty-nine days. "Can you help me, Carl?"

His reply was intriguing. "I can under one condition, Vincent. You either meet the condition, or we don't work together."

SEARCHING FOR STARS

▶ **We all need mentors that we can trust to tell us the truth.**

▶ **Mentors can come from inside your business, your friends, your family, or outside your business.**

3 ★★★★★

ROLL UP YOUR SLEEVES!

Y ou either meet the condition, or we don't work together." Vincent pondered the words. Carl's tone wasn't threatening or demanding; instead, it was warm and inviting. "What is the condition, Carl?" he asked.

"In the fifteen years I've been helping people with their businesses, Vincent, the one clear indicator of success is this: the CEO has to be personally involved. If they assign it to their staff as a project, it is never truly successful. Are you committed to taking this on personally and championing it? If so, we can work together. If not, I don't believe I can help you."

One of Vincent's strengths was his ability to develop people, and one of his ways of doing that was to delegate tasks and projects to his team. It helped them think like a CEO and it often delivered better results than if he had told them how and what to do. Now Carl was challenging his thinking, specific to recruiting his top three people. With the short window of time to find talented people, he really could not outsource this search to human resources. He had to make this a priority. He agreed to Carl's condition on the spot. They agreed to meet in person the next Monday afternoon. That left eighty-five days to fill the three roles with A players... rock stars, as Carl called them.

As Vincent prepared for his meeting with Carl, he couldn't help but wonder what magic he had that he was confident they could meet the deadline that Donna had imposed. What did he know that Vincent did not know? Vincent wasn't so vain as to believe he knew everything, but he just couldn't see how they could do anything differently than what he had already tried and failed at. He was sure they could throw money at someone and hire him or her quickly, but without a serious vetting process, how could they be certain the person would be a valued contributor?

Not only did they need to find people with the right skills and values, but they had to do it fast. He thought about how he had been promoted into the CEO role by David. The three leaders that left Smyth Tools to become CEOs elsewhere were his peers at the time. Initially there was some tension when he was chosen for the role, but as he worked with his staff, the tension dissipated. They became a smooth, productive team. He treated them well and valued their contributions and gave them opportunities to be visible to the board, and outside of the company. He had no regrets. Now they were gone, and this was the first time he had to go outside the company to find talent.

The Process Begins

On Monday, July 22nd, Vincent met Carl in the lobby of the building. He had taken Carl's condition seriously and he wanted Carl to know it. He would not have his assistant escorting Carl back to his office. He would be a hands-on, active participant in all phases of the process. He was setting the tone for the engagement and wanted to show Carl that he respected him and his request.

As they turned the corner into his office Vincent asked Carl if he would like to have a cup of coffee and talk through the project. Carl declined the coffee and asked Vincent if he could get a tour of the facility. After removing his sport coat, and donning a hard hat and glasses, Carl followed Vincent onto the manufacturing floor. Vincent was well liked and respected by the team doing the work of making their products. They knew he had started on the ground floor, although at another company. He spoke their language and he valued their input and the great work they did. When they saw him, they would smile and wave. Occasionally, as their work permitted, they would shake his hand or greet him with a comment or two. Usually the comments had some form of humor—a sign of true respect.

They were curious about who Carl was, but they also trusted Vincent, so they were not concerned. They could see Carl had a presence about him. He showed a true interest in the work they were doing and in them. When they would stop to talk to Vincent, he would introduce Carl as a friend who was going to help them find their new leadership team. Carl would shake their hand, look them in the eye and smile. They felt his curiosity and his respect as well. He would ask questions about their processes. He asked questions about how long they had worked at the company. Then he asked the question that was what he was working to define: "Why do you like working here?"

After the plant tour, Carl asked to visit with the office staff. He started with the finance department and worked through the same routine of understanding their processes, understanding how long they had been with the company, and why they enjoyed working there. Vincent could see the pattern. Carl was working to understand the culture of the company.

They had visited operations and finance, and Carl suggested they meet with the sales team. Most were in the field already, but the inside sales team members were available, and Carl spent time with them as well. He talked with each seller and worked the same process. Once he had spoken to each, he asked to meet and speak with the support staff. Carl had a way about him. He was warm and caring and people opened up to him quickly. He was able to get a feel for the culture of Smyth Tools in two hours of walking and touring and speaking with all associates. He seemed to value input from everyone, not just the managers.

When Vincent and Carl returned to Vincent's office, Carl took him up on the offer for a cup of coffee. They sat at Vincent's small conference table and they began the conversation about the challenge that they were working on.

Values First

"I love the culture you have created here, Vincent. The associates I spoke with love their jobs, love the company, and respect and trust you."

Vincent was taken aback. He was not used to getting this type of praise and he quickly tried to deflect the compliment.

"It really is a culture built by David; I just was fortunate enough to be the next in line."

Carl looked at Vincent thoughtfully and in his direct manner he said, "Don't deflect a compliment, Vincent. You earned it and you need to own it. This environment, this culture is a great differentiator when you are looking at filling the three roles. You will be a big reason that someone will want to join this company. You need to understand that. You also need to protect that. If you hire someone who doesn't have the same values as you have built here, they will become a cancer to your company. Again, you need to own it. Now let's get started."

Outcome Defined

"Let's define the finish line. What does success look like for you?" Carl was easing into the process that he had worked many times before. He always started with defining success. It's hard work to grow a business, and to try do so without a vision of what success looks like is almost impossible. The day-to-day work of taking care of the associates, the shareholders, and the customers can cloud the vision. "If you haven't defined success, Vincent, you will never get there."

Vincent felt like the answer was obvious: hire three C-level executives in eighty-five days—a head of sales, a head of operations and a head of finance. But he knew there was more to the question, so he waited a bit before answering. What does success look like? He started to speak, more to himself, than to Carl. He liked to verbalize his ideas. It was how he thought as an extrovert.

 "I guess success looks like having all three hired in eighty-five days. It looks like three talented A players, rock stars if we named it, on board and ready to produce. The team would meld well together and work as a team for the benefit of the company. They would fit into and advance our culture. They would have the skills and competencies that we need and the experience we need."

Carl was taking notes. "Anything else Vincent?"

"Well, they need to have a strong work ethic and high integrity."

Vincent was starting to understand where Carl was taking him. He was helping him define success, so that he could take actions to get there.

Carl pushed a little more. "Vincent, at the end of the eighty-five days, what will you do to celebrate your success?"

Celebrate success? Vincent hadn't thought of that. In all the assessment tools he had participated in, rewarding others and himself was not something he ever rated highly on. It was not a preference of his. While he knew others valued rewards, it just wasn't what made him tick. Therefore, he wasn't one to hand out compliments without a specific reason. He felt good work was an expectation and people didn't need a soft compliment or award for doing their jobs. Now Carl was suggesting that he not only needed to create the vision for success, but also build in a reward for reaching it.

Again, Vincent needed to think it through verbally. "We could hold a company picnic to celebrate, although I'm not sure everyone would get excited that we hired a new executive team. We could give out cards for free coffee, I suppose."

Carl took notes but shifted Vincent's thinking. "What will you do to celebrate, Vincent? What will you do to reward yourself?"

This took it to a different place for Vincent. He really had focused on not getting fired, not on how he would celebrate. "There is a great resort near

Marble Falls called Horseshoe Bay. It's on Lake LBJ and there are golf courses, a conference center, and a hotel. For quite some time I've wanted to go there and just relax. I've never been able to do so. I'd like to take Maria there. She has been so supportive over the years. Maybe that is the reward."

Carl smiled. "Now you are getting there, Vincent. Wouldn't it be fun to take your new team and their significant others to a three- or four-day business retreat to Horseshoe Bay? You could team build, get to know them personally, and build your strategy for moving forward. Work a few hours in a day, then enjoy the resort."

Vincent smiled, too, with his optimism growing around finding the right people.

"Where do we start, Carl? When do we start?"

Carl looked Vincent in the eyes and held his gaze for a few seconds. "Right now, Vincent. Let me start by sharing something I learned in my earlier career as a business leader. I was in a similar predicament as you are now. I had lost two key leaders in my organization. I wasn't prepared, and my internal staff couldn't step up as yours has. It almost cost me my company. After that incident, I made a vow to myself and I share it with everyone I work with. Always be looking for stars, Vincent. Always be looking for stars!"

SEARCHING FOR STARS

► The values that build a culture are just as important as the skills and experience a candidate brings.

► Interviews need to identify as much about values as skills.

► Using an outcome-based end point helps define the plan to succeed.

4 ★★★★★

THE ALWAYS-BE-LOOKING-FOR-STARS PROCESS

lways be looking for stars," Vincent repeated. "I should look for talent even when I don't have an opening for them?"

Carl nodded his head. "That is why I remembered you, Vincent. I saw a talented individual, and I knew someday we would find a way to work together."

This made Vincent smile. It fit with his belief in people. He knew it wasn't a coincidence that Maria had remembered Carl, and Vincent had searched and found him. Good people attract other good people. "How do we get started, Carl? We have a short window to find someone. Do you know a good recruiter?"

Carl simply nodded again but told Vincent, "But that isn't where we start. Let's talk about the process from step one through hiring. Do you have an established process for finding talented stars?"

Vincent had to admit they did not.

"Let's build one, then." With that, Carl unbuttoned his shirt sleeves and rolled them up, signifying that now they were going to work.

The Interview Process

"Let's start with your interview process and work both directions from there. By both directions, I mean finding talent, and then hiring talent. The interviews are the middle part of the process," Carl continued. "When you find candidates, what is the process you take them through before you hire them?"

Vincent had to admit there really wasn't one. They didn't hire many at this level in the organization, and there wasn't a rigorous process. The human resources leader would copy the resumes of the people they were interviewing, and then hand them out to the people who would be in the office the day the candidates came in. HR would set the schedule, and then they all used the resume in the interviews to determine who the best candidate was. He was guessing, but thought they probably had around a fifty percent success rate in hiring middle managers.

The senior team had been together for as long as Vincent had been in the CEO role. This was new ground. He shared this with Carl.

"To clarify, you don't have a set process for interviewing, but do you have a set process around tracking interview results or doing background checks?" Carl asked.

Again, Vincent explained that they did not. To his credit, he didn't get offended and try to defend the lack of process. He hired Carl to help and he needed his expertise. He had eighty-five days to hire three key executives. There was no room for ego.

Finding Rock Stars

"When you are interviewing the candidates, what are you looking for?" was Carl's next question.

Vincent had to admit they didn't have a clear vision of what they were looking for, or how to go about asking the right questions to get the answers. They had built money into the budget to cover the turnover they encountered, so they had never viewed it as a problem until now.

His answer to Carl's question was simpler, "We look for someone with industry experience. In fact, we hire away from competitors if we can."

"How do you find the competitors' people? How do you attract talent, Vincent?"

Vincent answered, "We let our HR team find them most of the time. I reach out to my network, or we run ads, or we find them through LinkedIn. But I must admit, I'm not really involved in that step."

"In our initial conversation Vincent, I stated that for me to work with you on this, you had to fulfil one condition, do you remember what it is?"

Vincent nodded and said, "Yes, I have to be personally involved."

"Are you still willing to do that? I'm not suggesting you must do all the work, but you must build and manage the process.

You must be hands-on."

Vincent agreed. He was willing to get deeply involved.

The Process

"Let me lay out the process, as I see it, and we can determine if it fits you and your company. First, we need to determine what skills or competencies you are looking for, by each role. I'm certain you have already defined your values, but we need to check to see how those fit into the interview process as well.

"There are four areas to determine fit with a company and a role: Does the candidate have the skill to do the job, the values that fit with your company, the experiences that show he or she has the will to do the job, and the aptitude for this type of work? In a well-planned, structured interview process, you can determine three of the four. You will need an aptitude assessment to get at the fourth."

Carl was beginning the teaching part of his offering to Vincent. He continued, "We will utilize multiple sources to find the right candidates. I'd suggest we tap our current associates to see if they have someone they could recommend. We can reach out to your network, we can create postings on other boards, but I've found LinkedIn to be invaluable."

With this, Vincent interrupted. "Carl, I've done that without any candidates coming forward."

Carl asked, "Did you post a job description on the boards or share the job description with your network?"

"Absolutely," Vincent responded.

Carl smiled and gave Vincent an inquisitive look. "Is that how David attracted you to this company?"

He had to admit that it was not. He explained how the recruiter that contacted him had shared a job description but had also spent time "inviting" him to be a part of the company. She had shared the vision that David had for the role. She explained the vision for the company, and while he was a little guarded initially, the invitation he received was compelling and he began the process of being interviewed and interviewing the people at the company so he could determine if they were a fit for him. He shared his thoughts with Carl. "A job description itself would not have attracted me. I see your point, Carl."

Carl continued his outline of the process. "We create an invitation to interview with a great company with a great culture. With that, we attract the right talent— those A players you are searching for. People want to help you, but you must be clear on what you are looking for. Whether you are asking your associates, your network, or a recruiter to help you,

you must have clarity on who you are searching for."

"Vincent, we have covered a lot of ground today. I want to be careful not to overload you with too much information at one time. Can we regroup first thing tomorrow morning?"

Vincent quickly agreed to clear his calendar for the morning. He would have eighty-four days to get this done.

Carl asked Vincent to set him up with a hotel near their facility, and Vincent had his assistant make the call.

"Can you think of who should be a part of the meeting tomorrow? We need input from a group of peers for the people we hire, and perhaps a representative from the team that would work for the new hires. We need a group of stakeholders who can help us build the skills and values matrix that we can use in the interview process."

Vincent made a note to set the meeting attendee list. "Tomorrow we start building the foundation for hiring stars for Smyth Tools."

It had been a long day, but Vincent was energized as he drove to his home. While they were still building the foundation and the clock was ticking, he felt he saw a way to accomplish his goal. Maria was in their study when he walked into the house. The kids were out with the neighborhood kids. It gave he and Maria a chance to debrief the day. He told of how Carl asked questions to help him understand where they had shortfalls in their hiring process. He explained the process Carl laid out for them to follow, and how he had reminded Vincent of his commitment to be involved in leading the process. "I believe this process he is talking about will be something we can use across the entire company, not just for the executive team. I'm excited. I believe we can meet Donna's threat."

Maria was happy to see Vincent's excitement. She knew his determination and drive. If he believed, he could make it happen.

Skills and Values

The next morning Vincent and Carl sat in the CEO's office, sipping coffee. Carl laid out his thinking for the meeting that was going to start in sixty minutes. "You have three key roles you are looking to fill, Vincent. Did you enjoy working with the people who were in those roles previously? What were the competencies they displayed?"

They started with the finance head. Vincent liked the reporting he produced and his ability to "see the future." He liked how he was a team player, and not just focused on the numbers, but how they could invest in areas that would allow them to grow even stronger. He had a sixth sense about what could be profitable and what would not. They moved on to the head of operations, then the head of sales, and there was a commonality in what he considered to be their strengths. They were strategic, and they focused on the business, not just their function in the business. It made him a little nostalgic for his old team, but that was a wasted emotion right now.

Carl next asked Vincent a question he had not thought about. He was reversing the order. "What does a successful sales leader do a year from now?"

Vincent had to give it some thought. After a brief pause to gather his thoughts, he plowed in. "First, they need to have a fully trained and functional team that produces the revenue and profit we are looking for. They need to be able to forecast accurately, and they need to be able to see the needs of the customer for new products, and perhaps new services."

Again, Carl was busy taking notes. After he worked through the same process with the other two roles, Carl paused for a minute. "Vincent, you have a very strong and supportive culture here. What are the values that you have as a company that make it so strong?"

While most companies have marketing materials or posters stating the values of the company, many companies do not live by them. They are just wall art. At Smyth, that was not the case. They lived their values. Everyone knew the five company values by heart, and they held themselves and each other accountable to them. Vincent shared them without looking for them. He knew them by heart.

"Are there any other things beyond the five you listed, that if a candidate doesn't live by them, you won't hire them?"

Vincent shook his head. With that, Carl shared the process he would take the team through at the meeting. He would facilitate a brainstorming session and capture the input. From there, he would take the input back to his office and convert it to skills and competencies.

The meeting included key people from each function of the business. They brainstormed in a round robin format until each idea had been exhausted. There was no debate on the advice, just an occasional question to clarify. After a little less than two hours, they had a large list of opinions on the skills needed.

Carl then laid out a suggested interview process for the candidates that came forward. It included telephone and in-person interviews in a timely, planned process that allowed the interviewers to be aware and have time to prepare. Carl suggested that after he had converted the input to skills and competencies, he would put them in front of the group for any suggestions. Once they agreed, he would build a format with interview questions and results tracking that they could use to take their candidates through the process.

After the meeting, Carl and Vincent sat down to debrief and talk through next steps. They agreed to meet again via video conference in three days. Carl was confident that he could have the documents ready for review by the team at that point. Carl packed his briefcase; they shook hands, and he left for the airport.

Distractions

An hour later, Vincent's cell phone buzzed. He recognized the number as a recruiter he had spoken to several times. The recruiter was friendly and never pressured Vincent. Vincent had talked to him every couple of months and he always seemed to have a role that he wanted him to interview for. While he wasn't searching for a job, he still had to think about his future and the threat from Donna. All this ran through his thoughts as he slid the icon to accept the call.

"Vincent, how are you doing today?" the recruiter began the call. "Can we talk about another opportunity?"

Vincent didn't know why he chose to share his situation with this individual, but he felt he could trust him, and he needed another person to share it with besides Maria. He told of Donna's threat, and he shared how Carl was helping him.

"The process he is working with you on sounds terrific, Vincent," said the recruiter. "If all companies would do that, it would make their job and mine much easier. You said you were in a search for a head of finance. I believe I have a candidate that you would really like. He seems to be a good fit for your company. Would you have interest in talking to him?"

Vincent saw an opportunity to shortcut the process. If he could find his finance person that would take some of the pressure off. "Let's set it up. How quickly can you have him here?"

The recruiter promised he could have the candidate in Vincent's facility on Thursday. They agreed to talk after the interviews on Thursday evening. Vincent walked out to his assistant and had her set up the logistics for interviewing with several of the stakeholders who had attended the brainstorming session with Carl.

As he drove home that evening, Vincent felt satisfied that he was making progress, although he did have a nagging thought. "Are we any better prepared to interview this person than we were before we met with Carl?"

SEARCHING FOR STARS

▶ **Define your interview process first, then build recruiting to find candidates, and then the steps to hire the best fit for your company.**

▶ **Have a clear understanding of the skills and values you need for the candidate to be successful and build the interview questions to identify both within the candidates.**

5

PROCESS DISCIPLINE YIELDS SUCCESS

The nagging feeling was still with Vincent as he drove to the office the next morning. Were we prepared to interview this individual for the head of finance role? His conscious was saying no, but his ego and drive were pushing him to act. Grab the opportunity to shorten the process.

As he walked into his office his assistant handed him a piece of paper with the schedule for interviews on it. He saw that he would be talking to the candidate over lunch that she was having catered into his office. Attached to the schedule was the write up on the candidate that the recruiter had sent via email. On paper, the candidate looked like a good fit. He had the experience and came from the industry. He had been promoted several times at his past company, and it looked like he was ready for the next step in title and responsibility.

As the morning progressed Vincent was focused on the business and not the candidate. He was analyzing reports on productivity when his assistant knocked on his door.

"Are you ready for your lunch meeting?"

He realized he had not really prepared to interview the individual. He grabbed the recruiter notes and moved to his conference table for lunch and the interview. As they talked through lunch, Vincent walked through the candidate's history and talked about where he wanted to take his career in the future. Vincent realized that he really had nothing to compare the candidate against. Without a clear understanding of what they wanted in the role, he was just wasting his and the candidate's time. After they finished eating, they stood, shook hands, and the candidate departed the office.

Vincent looked at his notes from the interview. He decided to act quickly and asked his assistant to gather all the team that had done the interviews. As they assembled in his office there was small talk about the candidate, but nothing of real substance. Vincent asked them to sit down at his conference table and he began the debrief.

He started with the acting head of finance. "What did you think of the candidate?"

The answer was short. "I liked him. He was nice and I think I could work for him."

Vincent pushed on. "What did you like about him?"

Her response was not as deep as Vincent had wanted.

As he went around the table the team had similar thoughts, but they really had nothing to support the fact that they liked the candidate. That nagging feeling that they were unprepared, himself included, came rushing back to Vincent. He needed to talk to Carl. He needed to do so before he spoke to the recruiter that evening.

Vincent thanked the team for their help in interviewing, and the group stood to leave the office.

"Are you going to make him an offer?" asked his acting head of finance.

"No. I don't believe we really know him. Liking him isn't the same as understanding his qualifications. I don't think we have a strong enough process to determine that he is the best candidate for us."

After the office was empty, Vincent picked up the phone and called Carl.

The Second Condition

Carl answered on the second ring. "Good afternoon, Vincent. I was just thinking of you." Vincent smiled and immediately felt a little better. Carl was there to support him, and he made Vincent feel more confident, just in speaking with him. Carl went on to share that he had completed his work on the competencies and values and was getting ready to send them to Vincent, ahead of the scheduled video conference.

Vincent shared his story of the call with the recruiter, and the subsequent interview with the candidate. He shared the nagging feeling that they weren't prepared.

Carl paused to gather his thoughts and see if Vincent wanted to add anything else to his story. The silence was challenging for Vincent. He felt some shame. He felt he had disappointed Carl.

Carl started with a statement and ended with a question. "Vincent, it is not unusual for a leader to get excited and want to take action immediately. I understand you're driven to succeed, and that is what has helped you get to the role you are in and the success you have with your company. Your drive is a strength if it is used skillfully. Was your drive skillful or was it unskillful in this event?"

That initiated a different thought process for Vincent. It was not good or bad behavior. It was about skillful use of his strengths. He appreciated Carl's question. "Carl, it was unskillful. I wasn't prepared to interview. We didn't have the competencies and the values to measure the candidate against. We wasted his time, and our time. It just wasn't productive."

He went on to tell Carl about the debrief session and the lack of detail in what the team liked about the candidate.

"Liking someone is not a competency we measure, Vincent. We certainly want to like the individuals we work with but using that as the criteria for hiring leads to turnover." He added, "We have one condition that we agreed to for us working together. I'd like to add a second condition; you need to agree that we will not shortcut the process. That actually lengthens the time it takes to hire, not shortens it. Do you see that now?"

Vincent agreed with Carl's second condition immediately.

Finding Rock Stars

"Let's use your strengths skillfully. Here is what I would suggest your next steps are." Carl shared the competencies and values with behavioral interview questions that supported the interview process that they had outlined in his earlier visit to the Smyth Tools office. He shared the invitation to work at Smyth Tools for Vincent to utilize to find Star candidates. Each invitation was specific to the role they were hiring for.

He suggested that Vincent take the competency and values matrix, along with the invitations, and share it with the interview team for their feedback. Once he had their input, they could tweak them as needed.

Then he asked Vincent to share it with his entire company, his network, and to send it to likely candidates through a targeted search using LinkedIn. He also suggested he post it on their website.

Finally, he asked Vincent to determine who would be the best recruiter to work with for each role. He could invest in a retained search with a focus on quality candidates in a short window.

Vincent had connected with Jeff, a phenomenal person, and recruiter from Chicago at one of his panel events earlier that year. He liked Jeff's detailed orientation around a search and his creativity. He had used him right after he met him. He and Carl agreed that he would be the person Vincent utilized.

As he ended the call with Carl, Vincent was more confident than he had been in some time. He realized he had tried to shortcut the process and had hurt the productivity of the search, but he learned from it and was ready to move forward.

He spent the next twenty-four hours executing on the suggestions Carl had urged him to take. He reached out to his close personal network with a very clear description of what he was looking for. He sent an email to the entire company with an invitation to offer candidates for the roles, with the promise of a $2500 bonus to the associate if they hired one of their referrals. He contacted Jeff and began the process of hiring him for the search. He was very focused on the competencies and the values the candidates must have, and he shared with Jeff the rigorous process that the internal team at Smyth Tools would take.

They were deep into the process. It was sixty days from the deadline Donna had given Vincent, of which she reminded him weekly. He felt they were making progress at a pace that he could hit the date. He had a slate of candidates for each of the roles.

What inspired him the most was that the candidates on the interview schedule came from multiple sources. Jeff had procured candidates for all three roles. In addition, a few of his top salespeople had referred Amy, who had competed with them in multiple opportunities. Some they won, some they did not, but her team was always professional and well prepared. Vincent's sellers respected that and suggested he interview her.

The head of finance interview slate included Mark. He came as a referral from Vincent's network. Mark had a reputation of having an uncanny knack for looking at a business opportunity and knowing whether it would be successful or not. He had a gift for taking emotion out of the equation, and using specific criteria, making outstanding business decisions.

Jeff had offered three candidates for the head of operations, but Brian stood out as the best on paper. He had a long track record of success with a large industrial distribution company. He had retired from the company, but was so young when he retired, he became bored.

The company brought him back, but it lacked the challenge he was looking for. Jeff felt Brian would be a great fit with Smyth Tools and Vincent, based on the very specific competencies and values that the team had developed.

The Interviews

Vincent again asked his assistant to set the logistics of the interviews. They dedicated an entire day to each role, with a slate of four interviewers, each with specific questions that were designed to uncover the abilities and values specific to the matrix they had built. The questions were assigned to each interviewer so there would be little overlap. The resumes were not offered. The team felt that they would be tempted to utilize the resumes, and that would be considered a lazy way of interviewing. They felt the interview process would differentiate them from the other companies pursuing the same candidates.

At the end of each day of interviews, the team would meet in Vincent's office to debrief and determine next steps for each candidate. The debrief was much more structured.

When he asked the acting head of finance for her feedback on the candidates, she started with "I liked them all" which drew a laugh because they had all been coached on "likeability is not a competency." She went on to explain in detail why she liked them, what numbers from their rating system she had assigned them, and what her recommendation was for each.

After they went through the process with each candidate, they agreed on who their final candidates would be. For finance, it was Mark. For operations, it was Brian. For sales, it was Amy. It now shifted to the final phase.

Checking References

The final phase was just as critical as every part of the process. Jeff took the lead on working the references for all three final candidates, even though Brian was his only person in the final group. The trust between he and Vincent had become just that strong.

Vincent would also check references. He looked to see if they had mutual connections through his network. He would reach out to them. They had a specific process for checking references that Carl had recommended.

After finding very positive responses to their inquiries on each of the three candidates, they set up the final interviews. The final interview was a "test drive" for each candidate. Carl had helped the interview team define a test for what would be a critical competency each candidate would need to be able to demonstrate. The intention was to see how they handled the test and what values they displayed. Carl was invited in for the last interview. The test drive was in a group setting.

Two days before the interview, each candidate was given the situation they would be addressing. They were to role play the situation with one of the interview team members, and the others were to observe. It went so well that the interview team unanimously agreed they should extend offers to Mark, Brian, and Amy.

After the team meeting, Vincent invited Carl to join him in his office. He was excited and energized by what they had accomplished and wanted to share it with Carl. While it wasn't finalized yet, he wanted to celebrate the process. He wanted to celebrate the steps they had taken to build a solid process to hire stars. His team had done an exceptional job. They had displayed the values of the company. They had the humility to learn and contribute to the process. They set aside the ego to build a better company—a better team.

After a quick recap with Carl, Vincent stood to shake his hand.

Carl congratulated him on a job well done. "Now let's bring it home, Vincent. Let's get these candidates hired and on the team." With that he turned to leave, but before he closed the door he turned and held Vincent's gaze for a moment. "People are the lifeblood of your company, Vincent. I know you are aware of that. Your investment of time and money in the project was substantial, but the return will be as well."

A few minutes later Vincent's telephone buzzed. He looked at the caller identification and saw it was Donna.

 "Vincent, the clock is ticking," said Donna. "I wanted to let you know that I've been conducting a search of my own, and

I believe I've found a suitable replacement for you. I'll be sharing it with the board at our meeting next month."

SEARCHING FOR STARS

▶ **Discipline around the recruiting, interviewing and hiring process is critical to putting every candidate on even footing so that you can identify strengths and weaknesses relative to your identified skills and values.**

▶ **Debriefs of interviews should be measured in a format that allows you to compare candidates and talk about specific skills and values.**

6

KEEP THE ROCK STARS HAPPY

Donna's threat had weighed heavily on Vincent's mind.

Vincent was sitting by the pool with Maria in the chair next to him. He was sipping on an IPA and enjoying the sunshine and warmth of the day. He had not really relaxed in several weeks— maybe months.

The stress of his team accepting roles outside the company, along with the stress from Donna and her ultimatum had been challenging. Now he had time to catch his breath and think of the lessons from the past and what he could take with him in the future.

Over six months ago, his finance, operations, and sales leaders had all been recruited away. He had worked hard to help develop their skills and help them grow into the outstanding leaders each of them is today. He was very happy for them and took some pride in their success. They were having great success as the CEOs of the new companies they had joined, and they spoke regularly.

He had the challenge from Donna. She threatened his leadership with the company. He will never forget the words, "Find replacements in ninety days or I will replace you!"

He would always be grateful for Maria's support. "Freeze, flight, or fight, Vincent. What will it be?"

He had fought, but not by himself. He had a great support network. His team at the company had worked tirelessly to keep performing while they searched for new leaders. He thought of his conversations with Carl and the insights he had gained. Carl had two conditions for working with him; he had to be personally involved, and couldn't shortcut the process.

They had built a strong recruiting and hiring process, starting with building clarity around what they wanted and needed in values and competencies. The process itself was rigorous and thorough. They had multiple candidates to choose from. They came from multiple sources. The people they hired had already made an impact in the business.

Rock Stars Produce

They had hired Brian as the head of operations. He was a great team member. He was an interesting person. He collected pinball machines, he drove cars he had modified on the track, and was a strong family man whose values aligned with Smyth Tools. He knew what levers to pull and where to focus his team. Productivity on the floor had increased by fifteen percent in less than three months of him joining the company.

Amy joined the company a week after Brian. She was more than just a sales leader; she was a brilliant strategist. She was outstanding at getting the best from her team. She could listen intently and make suggestions that were unique and effective. She balanced top line revenue with bottom line profit in a way few could. She and Brian had a strong connection which allowed them both to be successful. She also had the values they looked for. She was very proud to be the mother of two teenage boys who were outstanding athletes. She also was clear from the beginning that she would be involved with her family as much as she was in the business and she balanced them perfectly.

A few weeks later Mark had joined the company as the head of finance. Mark had been more difficult to hire than the others, but well worth the effort. He was very driven to understand the company, the market in which they served, and the opportunities that they were looking at. He was also focused on adjacent markets and the viability of expansion into those areas. It was the same skillset they had identified as a need when they built their competencies matrix. The way Mark worked through the interviews and the negotiations only furthered Vincent's desire to bring him to the team. He also had the strong set of values that they had identified. He had four very successful daughters that were living across the globe. Mark set his conditions early in the process. He and his wife would travel to see their family multiple times a year. He would work remotely, but he would need to have the freedom to travel.

It was important to Vincent and the company that this team would be a part of the family. Having a team with strong family connections was a part of the fabric of the company. Now here he was, sitting poolside in Horseshoe Bay on Lake LBJ in Marble Falls, reflecting. The team was becoming part of the Smyth Tools family.

Karma

A month after he had received the call that Donna had found his replacement, the board held their meeting. Vincent was asked to leave the room so that Donna could share her efforts to replace him with the board. Two hours later Vincent was called back into the boardroom. Donna was not in the room.

David took the lead. "Vincent, we are extremely sorry you had to work under these conditions. Please realize the board had no idea this was happening. We were all quite taken aback when Donna shared the conditions she had put you under and the fact that she had been conducting interviews for your replacement. We are extremely pleased with your performance and the performance of the company. You are family, Vincent—even though your last name isn't the same as ours, you are family!"

With that he congratulated Vincent on his hiring of the leadership team and the plans to finish the year.

A week later Smyth Tools offered a press release sharing that Donna had resigned from the board and there would be a search for her replacement. They would be looking to add two directors from outside the family. Replacing Donna as Chairman on an interim basis would be the founder, David. Internally, the intention was to groom David's youngest daughter, Dee Dee, to become the Chairman. David recognized his mistake in putting someone in the role that didn't share the vision and values of the company.

Dee Dee shared his vision and his values, plus she had grown up in the business. She was curious and was well-known and respected throughout the company.

Celebrating Success

Vincent took another sip of his beer. As he sat his glass back on the table between his and Maria's chairs he caught her looking at him.

"What?"

Maria smiled. "I'm so proud of you! You are a fighter, Vincent."

He realized that she also had felt the pressure from this experience, but as always, she had held down the home front with grace and dignity.

"I could not have done any of this without you." It was a team effort. She had been so supportive of him. When he was struggling, she knew how to challenge him with the right tenor. He was grateful for her belief in him.

Vincent suggested they needed to get ready for dinner. In an hour they would be hosting a dinner for Amy, Mark, and Brian, along with their spouses. It would be the first time the eight of them would be together, and they wanted to be able to spend time with each person, getting to know them as individuals.

They had a long weekend ahead of them. They had a dinner this evening, tee times tomorrow and Sunday, and a few hours of work on Monday, before they drove back to Houston. They each had openings in their staff, and they needed to define the competencies for the roles. Vincent was committed to the process. He would personally be involved, and there would be no shortcuts. This was going to be fun!

SEARCHING FOR STARS

▶ **Defining success before you launch the project allows you to know when you reach it and celebrate it. It rewards the hard work it takes to reach your goals.**

▶ **Having a clear understanding of competencies and values needed allows you to hire the best fit for your company. It improves your odds dramatically.**

APPENDIX A

Interview Process Suggestions For A Short Timeframe

Screening call

- Utilize set questions

- Ratings noted

- Move them forward or end process

Telephone interview, hiring manager

- Utilize set questions

- Ratings noted

- Move forward, send preinterview questionnaire, or end process

- AVA preference assessment sent

- Feedback to recruiters

In-person interviews, hiring manager, general manager, operations manager (cross functional)

- Utilize set questions for interview based on aptitude assessment test results and interview notes

- Hiring manager skills and competencies interview

- GM and operations, values fit, and cultural questions

- Ratings noted

- Move forward, or end process

Final interview and test drive, hiring manager, GM, and VP, HR

- Utilize set questions for interview, based on AVA results and interview notes

- Utilize set process for test drive/ role play

- Hiring manager, GM, VP, HR act as customers

- Ratings noted

- Continue process or end process

Reference check, hiring manager

- Background check, HR

Onboarding, based on process created, hiring manager leads the onboarding

APPENDIX B

Process Suggestion For Defining Skills And Values

Define what success looks like for the role

- After the new hire is in the role for one year

- Daily activities that lead to success

- The skills and competencies defined by the stake holders for the role, through a roundtable brainstorming session.

Create list of skills and competencies from input on what success looks like after one year, and the daily activities that lead to success

- The leader is responsible for conversion to skills and value

Define what values are critical for working for your company

- These are not skill based, but values based, i.e., integrity, work ethic, positive attitude, etc.

- If the candidate doesn't have 100 percent alignment with your values, you shall not hire!

APPENDIX C

Build Behavioral Interview Questions

Questions should correspond with the skills and values

- Assign specific questions to each interviewer at specific phases of the process.

- Create a numerical measurement system for tracking interview results by candidate.

- Debrief after each round of interviews to determine who continues in the process.

APPENDIX D

About The Author

Jerry Phillips is the president of NineRuns. For more than fourteen years he has been helping companies optimize and maximize the performance of their sales and marketing teams, shorten sales cycles, and increase close rates. In working with his clients, he has focused on having the right talent to execute on their selling operational strategy.

As an experienced business leader, Jerry held several key executive management positions. With his teams, he has driven results in sales, product development, marketing, operations and recruiting. He has created strategies to turn around underperforming businesses and developed the specific action plan for execution. He has extensive experience in both conceptualizing and implementing innovative solutions and processes for sales and marketing with Black & Decker/ DeWalt, Grainger, and Cold Spring.

Jerry and his team's dominant focus is helping companies build exceptional organizations that produce sustainable, predictable revenue with solid profit margins. They help develop strategy and execution plans and create and teach processes for consistent and predictable performance.

Jerry has written more than one hundred articles and has published two books on the recruiting process and has been quoted in Forbes. He is a recognized content expert in strategy, people performance, sales process, coaching, and defining and leveraging differentiators. He holds a B.S. in Business Management from LaSalle University in Mandeville, Louisiana.

Jerry enjoys living in Austin, Texas with his wife Jean and his dog Bo. He is avid about fitness and golf, although he is a total hack at golf.

Jerry can be reached at jdphillips@ nineruns.com or at 512.350.1536.

www.nineruns.com

APPENDIX E

Acknowledgements

This book is a work of love of business and for finding the right people for the right roles. None of this would have happened without the support from great mentors, great friends and a great family.

Thanks to my mentors, Dale (Mac) McCormack, the best leader I ever knew in my business life, and Carl Woods, the best leader I ever knew in my personal life. Thanks to Henry DeVries for the coaching and editing. Thanks to Jeff Hyman, whose book *Recruit Rockstars*, along with my recruiting experiences at Black & Decker, inspired me to build the process I use with my clients. Thanks to Mike Palm for being my resource for great insights in Marketing. Thanks to Jaclyn Miller who drops everything to help me with projects and research.

Bob Peck III has helped me to be a better writer and golfer (mainly writer—I'm still a hack at golf). He has encouraged me along the way and is direct and to the point in his feedback. I also want to recognize John Allenbach, Patrick Tate and Russ Alves. These three, along with Bob, are my brothers. We have "grown up" together and they have been friends through great success and monster failures. Thanks to Vince Cipresso for allowing me to loosely base the main character of the book on him.

I owe a great deal to my family for the support they have given me, not only on this book, but in the five major geographical moves we made as my career advanced. Jean Phillips has been an amazing partner in life and in supporting me in my business. Jeremy Phillips and Jessica Bookman have served as great inspirations on what the next generation can do. They both married well (Kelly Phillips and Max Bookman) and are providing me with beautiful grandchildren in Ellie and Colton. They all are rock stars.

I love fables. They provide a sense that if you work hard, have a positive approach, and do the right things, the ending will be happy. I've learned that this is how real life works, too.

READY TO HIRE STARS NOW?

ATTRACT ▶ RECRUIT & HIRE ▶ MANAGE & DEVELOP ▶ RETAIN

Hire Stars Now (HSN) is a Software-as-a-Service solution that helps guide you through a hiring lifecycle that will deliver stars.

The HSN solution helps you define the skills and values for each role, and guides you through a process to attract, hire and develop candidates that fit your needs as a company. The HSN solution offers out-of-the-box eight customizable business functions to choose from. The functions include Sales, Marketing, Product Management, Finance, Operations, Engineering, Customer Service, and Human Resources, both as an individual contributor and as a manager.

We help you define what success looks like for the individual and manager role, help you attract and hire the person who fits that role, and then help your hires execute a winning sales strategy following the **7 SalesSteps Strategy and Execution** process. The process greatly improves your odds of hiring the right person for your company and setting them up to perform.

Please visit **www.hirestarsnow.com** for additional details and take a test drive!